Original title:
Palm Tree Shadows

Copyright © 2025 Creative Arts Management OÜ
All rights reserved.

Author: Natalia Harrington
ISBN HARDBACK: 978-1-80581-599-0
ISBN PAPERBACK: 978-1-80581-126-8
ISBN EBOOK: 978-1-80581-599-0

Vows of the Verdant

In the breeze, they say 'I do,'
Leafy whispers, a crazy crew.
Promises in the summer air,
Dancing leaves without a care.

Sun-kissed hats and grassy shoes,
Napping hues in funny blues.
The vows are funny, who could tell?
As roots all laugh, they bid farewell.

Twilight's Gentle Caress

At dusk, the fun begins to flow,
Shadows stretch, they dance and grow.
Giggles echo through warm nights,
Coconut jokes and firefly flights.

Twilight wears a silly grin,
As crickets join the fun within.
Whispers of the day gone by,
With every laugh, the stars reply.

Cradled in the Shadows

Beneath the shade, I seek some peace,
But laughter bubbles, won't surcease.
Each chuckle dances in the air,
As sunbeams try to catch a fare.

Tickling toes of passing ants,
While squirrels practice silly dance.
The shadows tickle, and we fall,
Into a giggling, leafy ball.

Secrets of the Swaying

They share their secrets, oh so sly,
With rustling leaves and playful sigh.
A monkey winks, a squirrel's shout,
In gentle sway, they dance about.

The grass knows gossip, it's top-tier,
Of all the fun that happens here.
Banana peels and laughter loud,
In this green wonder, we are proud.

A Tangle of Leaves

Leaves up high play hide and seek,
Boys run fast, no time to peek.
A gust laughs, sends hats to flight,
Chasing them feels just so right.

Giggling as they duck and dive,
One fell down, "Oh, I'm alive!"
Sticks their tongue out, cheeky grin,
Nature's game, let chaos begin!

Memories in the Breeze

Whispers blow through branches wide,
Tickling your face, taking pride.
"Remember when we tried to dance?"
"With every twirl, we took a chance!"

Breezy tales of joy and fun,
Dancing shadows, oh what a run!
Echoing laughter, we've found our way,
In this funny, leafy buffet.

Layers of Reflection

Sunlight flickers through the fronds,
Like a painter's brush, it responds.
Ticklish toes on sandy ground,
Waves of giggles all around.

Mirror, mirror, on the sea,
Wait, is that a crab, or me?
If only life had more critiques,
Like how to dodge a seagull's beaks!

Twilight's Leafy Murmurs

As twilight falls, shadows dance,
Making friends with each glance.
A squirrel jives to a breezy tune,
While fireflies join; it's quite the boon.

Frogs in chorus, singing loud,
Competing with each echoing crowd.
"Did you hear that?" A laugh escapes,
Just wildlife trying fancy shapes!

Twilight's Green Veil

In the dusk, the branches sway,
A lizard winks, then darts away.
The coconuts have hats, it's true,
Like beachgoers, hiding from the dew.

The shadows dance, they laugh and tease,
A squirrel yells, "Hey, come and freeze!"
With every rustle, jokes unfold,
The leaves gossip, secrets told.

Secrets Beneath the Skyline

Underneath the leafy grin,
A monkey's plotting, where to begin?
He's got a stash of stolen fruit,
And plans to dance in a tiny suit.

The shadows stretch, they twist and curl,
As breezes swirl in a playful whirl.
"Why did the coconut cross the road?"
"To show the sea, it's quite the load!"

Sun-kissed Canopies

The sunbeams tickle, the leaves respond,
A parrot squawks, "I'm feeling blonde!"
With feathers bright and jokes to share,
He claims he's the king with the fluffiest hair.

Below, the shadows play peek-a-boo,
While crabs do the cha-cha, a funky crew.
"This dune's my throne!" they proudly proclaim,
In the world of shade, they're winning the game.

Reflections in the Shade

Mirrors of sunlight dance on the ground,
As iguanas strut, they spin around.
"Who wore it best?" they start to debate,
While flaunting tails, they sway with fate.

A tumbleweed rolls, it trips on a root,
While shadows laugh, "Nice dance, you brute!"
A lizard shimmies, bringing the charm,
"Join in, my friends, let's set off the alarm!"

Where Sunlight Dances

Beneath the sun, I lost my hat,
It flew away—imagine that!
A seagull caught it, what a sight,
He wore it proudly, what a flight!

Then there came a breeze so spry,
With laughter echoing from the sky.
A squirrel passed, a cheeky chap,
He winked at me, then took a nap.

Whispering Breezes of August

The wind's a giggle, how it plays,
With doggies chasing in the rays.
A kid on a bike, he zooms right by,
His ice cream lands—oh my, oh my!

Laughter bubbles up like soda,
As birds join in—a feathered moda.
A splashing wave, a watery call,
Could it be fun? Oh yes, it's all!

Shadows in the Warmth

In the heat, the shadows jump,
They dance like they're part of a thump.
A grumpy cat slinks in slow pace,
While tortoises race—what a funny race!

A picnic blanket bows and sways,
As ants form lines in quirky ways.
"Oh cheese!" they squeak, on a big old crumb,
A feast indeed, who'll have some fun?

Flickering Edge of Day

As sunlight starts to wear its dress,
A firefly twirls—it's quite the mess!
The evening chuckles with a glint,
While tiny shadows form a hint.

A crab tiptoes, with claws held high,
Pretending it's a superhero—oh my!
"Watch out!" it seems to shout and shout,
While seagulls giggle all about.

Whispers Beneath the Canopy

Underneath the leafy dome,
A squirrel steals a snack from home.
The birds gossip with much flair,
While ants march, unaware of air.

Lizards sunbathe, strike a pose,
In shades of green, they're quite the pros.
A breeze blows tunes, it's like a show,
As nature dances, to and fro.

Echoes of the Sunlit Grove

A monkey swings, so high, so free,
Chasing shadows, too quick for me.
The laughter of a child nearby,
Makes butterflies twirl, oh my, oh my!

Beneath the sun, the grass does tickle,
A crab calls out, its claws a pickle.
While bees hum tunes like jazz in bloom,
I trip on roots, and make a boom!

Silhouettes on Sand

Footprints lead where sand meets sea,
A crab winks back, quite mischievous he.
Seagulls squawk, like they own the place,
While I chase shadows, tripping in grace.

A child's giggle, a splash nearby,
The sun's the boss, how time does fly.
With buckets, spades, and a grinning face,
We build a castle, it's not a race!

Dappled Dreams of the Tropics

In the jungle gym of leaves so thick,
A toucan's beak does quite the trick.
Swinging vines like childhood games,
Nature's laughter, it never tames.

With every rustle, the stories blend,
Lifes' little hiccups, round every bend.
And as the sun dips, colors ignite,
It's a tangled web of pure delight.

Swaying Sentinels of Summer

In the breeze they dance with flair,
Beneath them, we play without a care.
They wave like kids on a sunny day,
Catching dreams before they go away.

With a bottle of sunscreen, we embrace,
While they wiggle in their leafy lace.
It's a game of hide and seek, you see,
Their shadows chase us, wild and free.

Oasis of Calm

Sunshine spills on the sandy shore,
Beneath those leafy giants, we explore.
Lemonade in hand, oh what a treat,
We giggle and lounge, tapping our feet.

They whisper secrets, tales of the sun,
While we feast on snacks, a whole lotta fun.
With humor in the air, we truly thrive,
As the leaves rustle, we come alive.

The Language of the Breeze

The whispers of wind do play a tune,
As shady giants poke fun in June.
They tickle our toes with playful glee,
While we laugh and dance, just like the sea.

In this symphony of shade, we're found,
With shadows acting silly, round and round.
Each gust a chuckle, a clap, a cheer,
In this funny world, there's nothing to fear.

Flickers of Time in Greener Realms

Time dances lightly, a jester in green,
With pas de deux twirls, a comical scene.
Shadows stretch out like a cat at play,
While we jump around, trying to stay.

Oh what a sight, on this sun-soaked stage,
As laughter erupts like we've turned a page.
With each little flicker, the moments extend,
In this world of fun, where giggles won't end.

Mysterious Tides of Dusk

As the sun dips low, the laughs arise,
Creatures dance beneath the swaying skies.
But what's that in the corner of my eye?
A crab's doing the cha-cha, oh my, oh my!

The flip-flops fly, a toddler on a spree,
Chasing shadows like they owe him a fee.
A seagull giggles at the scene so bright,
As shells conspire under the fading light.

A dog with time, he busts a sweet jig,
While beachcombers laugh at his funny wig.
A turtle, quite sly, with a shell that's a mess,
Mimics the moon, who clearly couldn't care less.

Oh, the tales that shadows begin to weave,
Spinning with humor, hard to believe.
Yet as dusk enshrines this kooky fest,
Laughter lingers long, an unwelcome guest.

Drifting Under the Golden Glow

Under the sun's warm, quirky embrace,
A duck does the backstroke, full of grace.
Nearby, a cat takes a thoughtful stroll,
Wearing shades, looking quite the cool mole.

The breeze teases hats, it plays them like flutes,
While kids zoom by on inflatable boots.
Their giggles echo, soft as a breeze,
While a crab flips sideways with elegant ease.

A couple in love shares a sandwich, oh dear,
A seagull swoops in, intentions unclear.
Fish and chips under the watchful eye,
Of strange, waddling pals, oh my, oh my!

But as day floats away on giggles and sighs,
The sun paints the sky with laughable lies.
Here in this space, where joy takes a bow,
Life's a carnival, come join us now!

Beyond the Escape

Beyond the woods, where shadows play tricks,
A raccoon is now plotting some silly mischief.
He entertains dreams of a night-time snack,
While a nightingale chirps, holding nothing back.

The moon takes a peek, stifling a yawn,
As fireflies twinkle, in a jolly dawn.
They giggle and dance on a breeze so sweet,
Leading lost socks to an inconspicuous seat.

A squirrel debates if it's cool to wear shades,
Complains about sunburn and unsightly fades.
With acorns aplenty and hilarious fuss,
He models his swag on the bus, oh, what a plus!

As darkness arrives with a comical twist,
The woods are alive; darling, you get the gist.
In this vibrant realm, let laughter abound,
Life's a merry-go-round, let joy be found!

Nature's Gentle Veil

In the garden where mischief blooms bright,
A rabbit in a bowtie prepares for a fight.
He's armed with a carrot, all fancy and spry,
Challenging flowers to duel, oh me, oh my!

The sunshine giggles as shadows entwine,
A worm in a top hat sips juice from the vine.
While daisies converse with giggles and grace,
Comparing their colors—who wins in the race?

A ladybug struts in its polka-dot gown,
Flirting with petals while wearing a frown.
A grasshopper boogies on a leaf from the lane,
Creating a party despite the light rain.

But as day turns to night, with stars in a whirl,
Nature laughs softly, as dusk starts to twirl.
Here in this garden, wild laughter prevails,
With echoes of joy wrapped in nature's soft veils.

Green-Hued Reflections

In the midst of swaying greens,
Where the lizards sing their tunes,
A squirrel juggles with his snack,
While I stare, and lose my whack.

The shadows dance, a silly show,
As dandelion seeds float, oh no!
A grasshopper leaps, then takes a bow,
I laugh so hard I spill my chow.

Underneath this leafy maze,
Mismatched shoes cause a gaze.
The shade's a stage, for blissful jest,
With giggles served as nature's best.

So bring your frolic and your cheer,
In this green world, fun is near.
Beneath the lush, the silly thrives,
And happiness will come in drives.

Dreams of a Canopied Night

Underneath the stars so bright,
I spot raccoons dressed for fright.
They waddle by with hats askew,
Planning mischief for a few.

The shadows wiggle, a ticklish tale,
A firefly joins the midnight hail.
With giggles echoing through the trees,
As families turn into buzzing bees.

Beneath the canopy, dreams take flight,
With whispers shared in pure delight.
A chorus of snorts from the furry crew,
Leaves me chuckling till morning dew.

So if you roam where shadows creep,
Join in the fun, let joyous leaps.
For beneath this leafy dome so vast,
Laughter and whimsy will ever last.

Serenade of the Canopy

A mariachi of crickets plays,
While fireflies flash in a funky haze.
The raccoon conducts with a flick of his tail,
As I sip my drink and start to bail.

Dance with me, oh rustling leaves,
Guide my footwork, if you please!
Twigs crackling like silly bones,
As laughter echoes in the groans.

The shadows waltz, a comical sight,
As I trip over roots in the night.
With each misstep, a chorus erupts,
The critters cheer; my flailing disrupts.

Beneath this canopy, let's let loose,
With tunes that'll make even mice deduce.
For in this dance, pure joy unfolds,
In shadows where fun and silliness molds.

Echoes of Reverie

A rustle here, a giggle there,
As shadows play without a care.
They toss my hat into the breeze,
And leave me swatting at the trees.

With each jump and crazy spin,
A deer snickers, what a win!
Dancing shadows on the ground,
In this fun fair, silliness is found.

Don't mind the raccoon with a grin,
He's just here to join the din.
Wobbling leaves in a masquerade,
Who knew that shadows could invade?

So gather 'round, embrace the cheer,
In echoes where laughter draws near.
With whimsy found beneath the boughs,
Join in the fun, and take a bow.

Echoes of the Tropics

Beneath the sun, a dance so bright,
Lizards play tag, what a silly sight!
With a flip of a tail, they dash and twirl,
Who knew reptiles could give such a whirl?

Coconuts drop, thud on the ground,
A surprise party, no guests around!
Monkeys giggle, sipping on zest,
Planning their heist, they're truly the best!

Hammocks sway with a lazy tune,
Dreaming of mischief beneath the moon.
Every swing's a chance for a pratfall,
The breeze can't stop these laughs at all!

In this paradise, we're saying, "Yay!"
Smiling at funny things every day.
With sunshine smiles, we all agree,
Life's a riot in this tropical spree!

Silhouettes in the Sun

Shadows stretch like dancers in jest,
Playing hide and seek, never at rest.
Every silhouette tells a tale,
Of battles fought with a sneeze, and a whale!

Sandy footprints lead to nowhere fast,
A crab thinks it's winning, but it's outclassed.
With a wiggle and jiggle, it scuttles away,
Chasing its shadow until the end of the day!

Sun hats fly off in the playful breeze,
Chasing after seagulls with such silly ease.
We laugh so hard, we might just fall,
Because chasing shades is the best game of all!

A sunburnt nose adds to the fun,
As laughter unites us under the sun.
In this silly world where shadows play,
Every moment's a giggle, come what may!

The Canopy's Embrace

Leaves whisper tales in a playful tone,
A squirrel drops acorns, claiming the throne.
With a leap and a bounce, it looks so spry,
But lands in a puddle—oh my, oh my!

Beneath the green, the laughter flows,
As beetles parade in their wiggly clothes.
Fungi hold meetings; oh, what a sight,
With cap-wearing mushrooms debating at night!

Swinging vines call with a mischievous pull,
Inviting all critters to dance, oh so full.
If you slip on a leaf, just giggle and grin,
Because nature's the stage where the fun will begin!

A canopy thick, with moments to share,
Each chuckle a treasure, floating in air.
With every turn, we find something new,
In this whimsical world where joy overflows too!

Swaying Secrets of the Breeze

The breeze carries secrets, oh what a tease,
It whispers sweet nothings to giggling leaves.
Twirling and swirling, oh, what a flight,
As crickets join in, chirping with delight!

A dragonfly zips, a sly little sprite,
Buzzing past sunbeams, oh, what a sight!
With a flip and a turn, it winks at a bee,
Both laughing at flowers that giggle with glee.

Our flip-flops clack as we race with glee,
Chasing shadows that bounce with esprit.
Every little stumble, a chance to unite,
In this dance of fun, where we feel so light!

As stars peek out, the mischief won't cease,
The night air is filled with such joyous peace.
With every breeze that drifts through the trees,
We join in the laughter; oh, what a tease!

Touch of the Tropical Twilight

Underneath the swaying fronds,
The sun plays trickster games,
Casting shapes like silly puns,
Where laughter wears no names.

Coconuts in awkward dance,
Bounce with the rhythm of the breeze,
Tell the tales of summer romance,
While monkeys sip their teas.

Sipping drinks with paper hats,
Waves of giggles roll ashore,
Squirrels sharing silly chats,
Who knew palms could bring such lore?

So let's toast to shadows bold,
Their antics never dull,
In twilight hugs, mysteries unfold,
A tropical merry hull.

Garden of Whispered Secrets

In a grove where secrets hide,
The shadows wiggle with delight,
Lizards take a goofy slide,
As they flaunt their craze in flight.

Frogs croak funky serenades,
While crickets join the show,
In this patch of leafy shades,
Nature's humor starts to glow.

Bananarama swings in fun,
As the breeze begins to tease,
Even flowers dance and run,
Underneath the leafy trees.

Whispers flutter like a song,
Each giggle softly gleams,
In this realm, we all belong,
Where laughter flows like dreams.

Light and Shade Serenade

Under swaying fans, I lose my hat,
A bird steals my snack; imagine that!
Sunshine tickles my toes so bright,
While squirrels dance in a comical fight.

Giggles echo in warm afternoon,
As shadows stretch like a lazy tune.
A lizard runs like it's late for tea,
In this sunlit circus, come laugh with me!

My iced drink melts like dreams in July,
A breeze whispers secrets, oh my, oh my!
Sunbeams wink, playing hide and seek,
Life's a joke on this vibrant peak.

With each giggle, the worries melt,
Under this shade, pure joy is felt.
So grab a beach ball, let's have some fun,
In this silly scene, we've only begun!

Tranquil Tropics

In the tropics, where coconuts sway,
I tried to dance, but slipped away!
A crab laughed hard and scuttled off,
As seagulls squawk like they're having a scoff.

The sun plants kisses on sandy toes,
While a lizard slides like it's putting on shows.
With every giggle, the day feels vast,
In this quirky paradise, life zooms past.

Tiki torches flicker, the night feels nice,
As everyone claims to be a great dice.
But rolling our laughter is the best of all,
In this cheerful chaos, we stand tall.

So join the fun, don't be shy,
There's joy to share beneath this sky.
In this tranquil place, let's dance and play,
As life brings jokes in the silliest way!

Dancing Leaves of Sunset

As evening falls, the leaves take flight,
Twisting and turning in awkward delight.
A squirrel's pirouette steals the show,
While the sunset paints the world aglow.

Twinkling stars begin their dance,
As fireflies wink, giving us a chance.
To twirl and spin with nature's beat,
While the moon giggles from her cozy seat.

Laughter rings as we kick up sand,
Chasing shadows like a merry band.
The night hums softly, a sweet refrain,
In this whimsical world, joy is our chain.

So join the frolic, lose your cares,
Under this sky, fun always dares.
With dancing leaves and a sunset fair,
Let's revel in moments, beyond compare!

Shadows on Sandy Shores

Shadows dance as the sun says bye,
While crabs perform fouettés for the sky.
My flip-flops fly with each crazy twist,
In this playful world, you cannot resist.

Sand castles rise, then crash with a laugh,
A rogue wave steals my body's giraffe!
We chase the tide as it pulls and pricks,
Life's just a joke, made up of tricks.

With giggles stretching, the ocean glows,
Surfers tumble like they've lost their prose.
In this sandy circus, let's join the spree,
With laughter and games, come dance with me!

So splash and frolic in this seaside crew,
With every wave, we find something new.
On this sunny stage with shadows galore,
Let's write our own tales forevermore!

Canopy Conversations

In the shade, the chatter grows,
Leaves gossiping as the sun glows.
Squirrels trading silly jokes,
While lazy lizards bask and poke.

"Hey, did you hear about the breeze?"
"Yeah, it tickles even the trees!"
They laugh and sway, such silly pals,
A circus of chatter under their pals.

Frogs croak in harmony and glee,
A concert whispered by the sea.
Oh, what a scene, what a delight!
Shade is the stage for laughter's flight.

With each rustle, a new tale spins,
Of sun-soaked afternoons and wins.
Who knew green could be so bright?
Underneath this canopy's light!

Seasons of the Sway

Spring brings jiggles, a dance so spry,
As branches sway and giggle, oh my!
Summer's heat, a lazy show,
Twisting arms in a sunlit flow.

Autumn leaves don their funny hats,
Dancing down, eluding spats.
Winter winks with frosty glee,
Swaying softly on a chilly spree.

Each season joins the merry fun,
Chasing shadows, but never done.
With laughter echoing in the air,
Their playful jig makes us declare!

What a circus in the sky!
With whispers low and high,
They sway and twirl, oh what a hoot,
A timeless jig in sunshine's suit!

Paintings of the Wind

A brush of air, a masterpiece,
Colors swirling, never cease.
Whispers carry tales of cheer,
As shadows dance, they disappear.

Every gust a laughing note,
In swinging song, the branches float.
Artistry in each gentle sway,
Creating joy in a lighthearted way.

Canvas of leaves, a bustling scene,
Dreamy shades of evergreen.
Who needs a gallery so grand?
When nature's brush is close at hand!

The wind creates, the laughter glides,
In this theater, fun abides.
With echoes bright, we all agree,
In this artwork, we're all free!

Notes from the Tropics

In the tropics, life is bright,
With every laugh, a new delight.
Coconuts joking, "Look at me!"
Swinging low, so carefree.

Parrots squawk in silly tones,
Juggling fruit, they steal the show!
"Catch my mango!" one would dare,
As laughter fills the humid air.

Under the sun, the fun won't stop,
With shadows playing hopscotch atop.
Every twig and leaf a friend,
In this laughter, joys blend.

So here's a tune from nature's band,
Swaying together, hand in hand.
With every note, the fun goes on,
In the tropics, we endlessly fawn!

Ethereal Shadows of the Isles

In a dance so light, they sway,
The shadows play hide and seek each day.
Under the sun's relentless grin,
They giggle as the day begins.

Laughter escapes from chubby coconuts,
As breezes tease the sun-warmed nuts.
With every sway, a flicker of cheer,
Aerial antics that draw us near.

Beneath the shade, we sip and sigh,
With a wink, the shadows like to lie.
They whisper tales of the foolish sun,
As we chuckle and bask, life's so fun!

So come along, join this merry trip,
Where shadows dance and our spirits zip.
In the quiet guffaws of golden bright,
We find joy in the silly delight.

Flourish of the Monsoon

Raindrops giggle as they slide,
On slick leaves where the secrets hide.
Each leaf's grin just triggers glee,
As puddles laugh, "Come jump with me!"

The wind throws fits, a playful rogue,
While clouds puff out with an airy vogue.
Nature's laughter fills the air,
As splashes echo everywhere.

With every wiggle, our socks go wet,
In dancing shoes, there's no regret.
The rhythmic drops create a song,
A jolly tune, where all belong.

So let it rain, let the chaos reign,
In wet delight, forget the mundane.
With each murmur of the stormy tune,
We'll dance and laugh, a goofy boon!

A Symphony of Fronds

The fronds perform a quirky jig,
While crabs in costumes prance and dig.
Banana peels slip, what a sight,
As they tumble down, causing delight.

Gusts of wind toss hats with flair,
While lizards play cards in open air.
With a twirl, the fronds like to shout,
"Watch out for that sneaky sprout!"

Chasing chirps and zany tunes,
Underneath the watchful moons.
Beneath the fronds' melodic sway,
We laugh and play the sunny way.

At day's end, when shadows blend,
We'll toast to joy with laughter's mend.
In harmony, the silly breeze flows,
A splendid mix that only grows!

Silhouetted Reveries

As daylight wanes, the sillies creep,
In shadows long, where secrets sleep.
The evening giggles begin to rise,
As dreams take shape in twilight skies.

Silhouette dances beneath the night,
With clumsy moves, oh what a sight!
Mistaken steps and bumping toes,
In laughter's grip, hilarity flows.

Stars twinkle like mischievous sprites,
In a comical show of starry lights.
The moon snickers at our goofy plight,
As we hug the darkness, held tight.

So let's embrace this shadowy scheme,
Where laughter lifts us, like a dream.
With every chuckle in the dark,
We weave joy's tapestry, like a lark.

Dance of the Shaded Hour

Underneath the leaf parade,
A critter's jam is well displayed.
They twist and twirl, with little care,
As breezes toss their furry hair.

A lizard moves like it's on fire,
With swagger that a cat might tire.
The ground's a stage, so slick, so neat,
Watching them, I can't feel my feet.

The shadows dance, they upbeat gleam,
Where sunbeams skip and giggles dream.
In this wild lawn, mischief's afoot,
With antics that are quite a hoot.

So join the fun, don't hesitate,
Embrace the shadows—it's just great!
With giggles bright and breezy cheer,
Dance with the critters, have no fear!

Verdant Veins Against the Moon

Up in the night, the leaves conspire,
To make the moonlight feel like fire.
With shadows cast in funny shapes,
The night seems filled with laughing apes.

A raccoon juggling fruits galore,
Swings from branches, seeking more.
The moonlight winks, it knows the scoop,
As creatures join the quirky troupe.

With every rustle, there's a cheer,
Are those dance moves? We can't be clear!
But who cares—just grab your drink!
Join the shenanigans, don't overthink.

So let's raise glasses to the quirks,
A night of laughter, wild jerks.
With verdant veins beneath the sky,
Let's dance until the stars all sigh!

Shade-Cast Memory

A squirrel's dance in the afternoon,
Beneath the leaves, a silly tune.
He drops a nut, then does a spin,
In search for treasures, where to begin?

The shadows stretch, they seem to prance,
Inviting all to join the dance.
With giggles floating in the air,
The bunnies hop without a care.

Oh, what a sight, this grassy fun!
Glimpsing mischief, making a run.
A shadow lands, like a playful flick,
In a game of tag, it does the trick.

So here's to laughter, wild and free,
As shadows weave their history.
In this moment, let's all share,
A shade-cast memory, beyond compare!

Waves of Green

The grass does sway like ocean's tide,
With critters surfing, full of pride.
A beetle glides on blades so tall,
While grasshoppers dare to take a fall.

The shadows hide what's underneath,
A treasure chest of funny wreaths.
A worm in shades, he struts about,
His moves could make a dancer pout.

And look! A snail joins in the race,
Waving slow, with utmost grace.
The green waves crash, and laughter sings,
In this garden, joy takes wings.

So let's all dive in joyful leaps,
Where the humor grows, and nothing sleeps.
With waves of green that whirl and sway,
Join in the laughter, come what may!

Elysian Echoes

Underneath the sun's bright grin,
Giant fronds sway, where laughs begin.
Monkeys swing in a clumsy way,
They trade their snacks for a fun-filled play.

Tropical breezes steal my hat,
Every gust a playful spat.
I chase the breeze, the hat in flight,
With all my might, I join the fight.

Laughter echoes on golden sands,
Seagulls joke with their tiny bands.
In their chorus, I sneak a tease,
"Hey! Who's the real bird that flies with ease?"

When shadows stretch beneath the sun,
I swear the coconuts just run!
A coconut rolls like a bowling ball,
I can't resist, I laugh and fall.

Compositions of Light and Dark

Sunlight dances, the shadows play,
Straw hats wobble, what a display!
The crabs march sideways, quite absurd,
Each step a jig, as if they've heard.

A shell tosses in the salty breeze,
Where's the punchline? I'm left with tease.
The sun shines bright, the shadows tease,
Why do they always seem to freeze?

Beachgoers stumble with glee abound,
Sand between toes makes laughter sound.
A slip, a trip, oh what a sight!
It's comedy gold, day and night.

Laughter spreads like a sunbeam ray,
Echoing on this tropical bay.
In this moment, how can I tell,
If I'm laughing at me or at them too well?

Ghosts of the Isles

In the twilight, spirits dance,
With flip-flops on, they take a chance.
Haunting jokes, as shadows loom,
They float around, making me fume.

"Why don't you float?" I chime aloud,
A ghost replies, "Not in this crowd!"
With a wink, they vanish from sight,
Leaving me chuckling; what a fright!

They whisper tales of lost treasures,
Pirate hats and silly measures.
In the twilight, they play charades,
Absolutely lacking in parades!

Then suddenly, with nary a sound,
The wispy forms twist all around.
"Dance with us, you footloose guy!"
I'd rather stick to my dance supply!

Footprints in the Lush

In a patch where grasses grow tall,
I leave behind my footprints small.
Laughter trails me, come join the quest,
Every step feels like a jest.

Bumblebees hum a silly tune,
While I twirl beneath the warm moon.
A frog croaks with a comic flair,
It leaps with style, as if it's rare!

A snail slips by, all slow and grand,
"No rush," it says, "I've got a plan!"
With shells on backs, they glide with ease,
I'm the one who's trying to tease!

Soon the sun sets, colors blend,
Bringing an end to this funny trend.
In the lush, where mischief reigns,
I'll return tomorrow for more silly gains.

Lullabies of the Green

Under the fronds, the shadows dance,
Tickling toes as they take a chance.
Laughter echoes in the warm sea air,
Swaying gently without a care.

A coconut drops, a playful thud,
Rolling away like a cheeky bud.
Sunlight streams, where giggles blend,
Nature's joke, around the bend.

Flip-flops fly; they've lost their way,
Caught in the breeze, in a game of play.
Shadows waltz in daylight's glow,
Beneath the green, the laughter flows.

So nap your worries, let joy abound,
In this silly, leafy playground.
The world's a stage where we all sigh,
For a little fun, we'll always try.

Guardian of the Island Light

A sunbeam rushes, a playful tease,
While goofy shadows dance with ease.
From morning till the day is gray,
Nature's giggle leads the way.

Beneath the shade, the beach balls fly,
And silly seagulls caw and cry.
Two kids race with ice cream stains,
Chasing each other, ignoring their pains.

The wind whispers tales from afar,
Of dancing stars and a beach bazaar.
With every gust, a funny tune,
As coconuts wink at the silly moon.

They nestle in, the mischief stirs,
Mirthful moments, laughter blurs.
Oh, guardian of our sunny plight,
Direct our joy, from morn 'til night.

The Embrace of the Breeze

The breeze arrives with a friendly grin,
Tugging at clothes, let the fun begin!
It dances soft, with a hint of sass,
Saying hello to all those who pass.

The laughter floats, a buoyant kite,
In shadows deep, where giggles ignite.
A pair of flip-flops are skimmed away,
As silly whispers bid them to stay.

Through tangled grass, we chase the light,
Spinning kids like a kite in flight.
With every gust, a new surprise,
Swaying leaves in a playful rise.

So let's embrace this breezy friend,
Joyful moments, never to end.
In the warm retreat where shadows blend,
Giggles and mirth, the laughter we send.

Leafy Lounging

Lounge in the shade, a hammock sways,
While critters plot their silly ways.
A squirrel slips, with a nut in tow,
Creating chaos, it puts on a show.

The sun laughs down, a playful guide,
While shadows stretch, no need to hide.
A picnic of laughter, all laid out,
With sandwiches shaped for a silly route.

Why did the leaf fall, what a jest!
To land on a nook and take a rest.
Giggling breezes tease and twirl,
A leafy world in a jolly whirl.

So let's lounge beneath the leafy cheer,
For laughter is best when friends are near.
In this whimsical nook, we can't refuse,
An endless game, where joy ensues.

Clusters of Grace

A bunch of fronds sways side to side,
With a cheeky grin they try to hide.
Whispering secrets to the sandy shore,
Wiggling their fingers, asking for more.

Sunbathers giggle in the warm sunlight,
As the shadows dance, what a funny sight!
Underneath, the coconuts conspire,
Messy drops cause laughter never to tire.

Lovers pose for selfies, arms held wide,
These leafy giants offer a silly ride.
Branches bending low, trying to tease,
Rustling like friends, "Oh, don't you sneeze!"

At sunset's glow, they hold a show,
Casting their shapes, a fantastic flow.
"Look at us all!" they proudly beam,
Nature's comedians, living the dream.

Beneath the Tropical Sky

A group of leaves with a wicked flair,
Telling tales of winds and salty air.
They sway and dip in a playful tease,
Chasing the sun, dancing with ease.

People drift in hammocks, lulled to rest,
While shadows tickle, a light-hearted jest.
Footprints mark the sand, where giggles grow,
As shadows stretch long and steal the show.

Children run wild, racing through the maze,
Dodging the shade in a gleeful craze.
Each brush with the ground, a spark of delight,
As the palms cheer on in their own sunlit fight.

With a wink and a wave, they send us a grin,
A reminder of joy that starts from within.
So grab a coconut, let laughter fly,
Under the gaze of a warm, smiling sky.

Mirage of Green Dreams

In the bright daylight, shapes intertwine,
Stretching and reaching in a line.
They flicker and flutter, a vibrant show,
Saying, "Come dance, join the fun below!"

Picnics unfold on a blanket spread,
With shadows leaping over the bread.
Lovers sip drinks while shadows flirt,
Splashing the scene with a dash of mirth.

Every gust of wind brings a new surprise,
Leaves crackle with jokes and sly little lies.
"Not too close!" they whisper in playful scorn,
As a rogue breeze ruffles a beach hat worn.

As dusk approaches and colors collide,
With laughter echoing, they stand with pride.
A goofy parade, shadows in sync,
Nature's jesters, always in the pink.

Elegance in the Glow

When the sun dips low and the sky ignites,
Shadows prance dressed in evening lights.
With a bashful sway, they twist and turn,
Creating a spectacle, watchers yearn.

All around, the chatter and cheer,
As the silly shadows begin to appear.
They circle the crowd with their quirky dance,
Giggling softly, giving chance a chance.

Sipping on drinks, toes in the sand,
While the green archers extend a hand.
"Join our party!" they seem to shout,
"Who needs silence when laughter's about?"

As stars awaken, the laughter ignites,
Shadows frolic, reaching new heights.
With every wave and every cheer,
An elegant glow, a joyful sphere.

Nature's Shaded Embrace

Under the leaves, where squirrels dance,
The sunbeams play, as if by chance.
A lizard slips, with style so bold,
Wearing a cloak of green and gold.

The shadows stretch, in goofy ways,
They twist and turn like kids at play.
A breeze suggests a cool retreat,
While ants compete to claim their seat.

With every rustle, giggles rise,
The frogs join in – what a surprise!
In nature's realm, silliness reigns,
Where laughter flows through sunlit lanes.

So join the fun, let spirits soar,
In this lush land, there's always more.
Here, under the sun's warm embrace,
Life's petty woes simply erase.

Beneath the Lush Canopy

Coconuts fall, a game of chance,
As tourists duck and start to dance.
The birds all laugh, with cheeky cries,
As we look up with wide-open eyes.

Beneath the greenery, mischief brews,
A monkey steals a flip-flop shoe.
We chase it down, a silly sight,
While reflecting on our travel plight.

The shadows wiggle, tease and play,
Making shapes in a fun display.
A hidden crab comes out to strut,
Claiming his prize, a half-eaten nut.

So here we are, in nature's zest,
Where laughter lies and fun's the best.
Let's take a break from the daily grind,
And see what joy we can all find.

Shimmering Silhouettes

Sunset paints the sky in gold,
While silhouettes make stories bold.
A dancing shadow, a curious cat,
Wanders around, what's up with that?

The surfboards lean, a playful crew,
As waves gossip, the sea's old hue.
A seagull squawks in jest, it seems,
Dreaming of fish in colorful dreams.

As night creeps in, the shadows grow,
The beachside bar's set for a show.
We drink from mugs with festive flair,
While dolphins giggle in salty air.

So join the fun, it's all in jest,
In shimmering shades, we are our best.
Let's make some memories, wild and bright,
Until the stars twinkle in the night.

Tales from the Tropics

Beneath the rays, the stories hum,
Of laughter shared, and endless fun.
The crickets chirp their evening tune,
While fireflies spark like stars at noon.

A wise old turtle takes his time,
Crossing the path, it's truly sublime.
He winks and nods, then tells a tale,
Of treasure maps and mysterious whales.

The breeze carries jokes from tree to tree,
As parakeets squawk in jubilee.
We join the gags and laugh out loud,
In this wild place, we're all so proud.

So gather round, let stories flow,
In tropic lands where humor grows.
With nature's touch, each moment's grand,
We'll keep the joy in every hand.

Floating on Green Whispers

Underneath a leafy dome,
Lizards prance like they're at home.
Coconuts make quite the sound,
As they drop on folks around.

Swaying high, they share their glee,
With every rustle, a loud tee-hee!
Birds chime in with silly songs,
As sunlight dances, all day long.

Fables of Fronds

Once a branch decided, 'Hey,
Let's host a party for the day!'
Breezes twirled and danced with glee,
While bugs joined in, a jubilee!

A squirrel tried to join their fun,
But slipped and fell, oh what a run!
The next guest was a cheeky hen,
Clucking jokes, 'Let's start again!'

A Dance of Dappled Light

Shadows jiggle on the ground,
As critters gather all around.
A frog leaps in a leafy hat,
Singing tunes, how strange is that?

The sun peeks out, gives them a wave,
While shadows copy, oh so brave!
A rabbit hops, a twisty fate,
Tripping into a leafy crate!

Essence of the Swaying Light

The breeze invites a playful swirl,
As brushy tails begin to twirl.
Bashful butterflies take a turn,
As sunlight teaches them to learn.

A hilarious scene's brewing here,
With laughter echoing, loud and clear!
In this sanctuary of cheer,
Life giggles softly, never fear.

Beneath the Fronds

Under fronds, I lost my hat,
A squirrel claimed it, fancy that!
He wore it proud, what a sight,
I laughed so hard, deep into night.

A breeze blew by, my drink went high,
It splashed a friend, oh my, oh my!
We chased it down, what a race,
In this wild chase, I fell on my face!

Sticky fingers, sandy toes,
Sunshine giggles, the laughter grows.
Later found a seaweed snack,
I chewed it once, then had to hack!

Beneath the fronds, life's a jest,
With silly moments, we are blessed.
So raise your glass, let's toast the day,
With laughter bright, we'll always play.

Serenity in Twilight's Embrace

In twilight's glow, a lizard danced,
I tripped on air, not quite by chance.
He blinked at me, quite unafraid,
As I flopped down, my plans delayed.

Bugs flew past, a zany swarm,
I waved them off, trying to charm.
But one lands soft upon my nose,
I squealed and fled, as laughter rose!

The sunset fades, the frogs all croak,
Their crooning jokes, no need to poke.
I clutched my sides, the night was young,
With silly songs, our hearts were strung.

Embraced by night, it's all a game,
We shared our stories, giggled the same.
In this calm air, the fun won't cease,
Together we troll, life's sweet release.

Shapes of Solitude

In solitude, I found a chair,
A bug decided it was fair.
He danced about, a silly show,
I clapped and cheered, my new best bro!

Sketching shapes on the sand's soft bed,
A fish swam by, so I pretended!
I drew a fish, it looked like dough,
He rolled away, just so I'd know.

Then clouds came by, in funny forms,
A cat, a hat, oh how it warms!
I laughed so much at this balloon,
Imagining others, flying soon.

Solitude was never bland,
With wiggles, giggles, just as planned.
Shapes of laughter are all around,
In every corner, joy is found.

Enchanted Leaves in the Breeze

Leaves giggle softly in the wind,
Whirling stories, they're my kin.
I chased one down, thought, it would stay,
But it twirled off, as if to say:

"Catch me if you can, oh what a tease!"
I tumbled and stumbled, couldn't believe!
The grass was soft, and so I fell,
With leaves all round, it's quite the swell!

A funny bird joined in the fun,
He squawked and danced, oh wasn't he one!
With flappy wings, he stole my snack,
I laughed so hard, nearly lost my pack.

The night approached, stars peeked bright,
In leafy company, all felt just right.
With whispers sweet and giggles loud,
We shared our secrets, free, unbowed.

Notes from the Edge of the Shore

The sun has danced away from noon,
As I try to nap, but I hear a tune.
A seagull squawks like a silly king,
As waves applaud and the crabs do swing.

The beach recliner's my throne, you see,
But seagulls plan a heist on my brie.
I chase them off with a flailing arm,
They laugh at me, but they bring no harm.

My sunscreen's a potion of great delight,
I miss my nose and now I'm a sight.
Friends call me lobster, I'm rather red,
But look at my drink! I'm feeling well-fed.

The sunset giggles, I join the spree,
With laughter echoing from you to me.
The shore might tease, just a bit of fun,
Tomorrow I'll conquer, or just eat a bun.

Gestures of Green in the Evening

Beneath a hat that's far too wide,
I wave at strangers like a crazy guide.
With drinks in hand, we spill and cheer,
Our antics echo as shadows appear.

A frisbee flies, but lands in a patch,
Of coastal grass—a great big scratch!
Was that a bird or a chubby cat?
We laugh and wonder, it's where we're at.

Someone trips over their flip-flops loud,
While clumsily trying to join the crowd.
But a tumble turns into a breakdance twist,
We cheer so loud, it's a moment not missed.

The colors fade, but we'll stay bright,
With laughter, we embrace the incoming night.
Tomorrow's antics wait on the green,
For now, let's dance, eyeing the unseen.

The Harmony of Light and Shade

With a cooler in hand, I set my scene,
A sandwich's whisper, all feels pristine.
But the moment I sit, a sandstorm starts,
Uninvited grains join my culinary arts.

The sun's a joker, bringing a tan,
While my towel's stuck to my soggy plan.
Under a sunhat that's three sizes wide,
I'm quite the sight, come take a ride!

My friends begin to lose their cool,
In their laughter, I find the golden rule.
We're all a mess, but such joy we share,
In this conga line of sun-kissed hair.

The light and shade play playful tricks,
Turning our selfies into magic clicks.
We toast to the quirks with our silly shade,
This comedy show, the best we've made.

Sunlit Dreams on Ocean's Edge

With my hat pulled low, I plot my day,
While seeking treasures washed away.
A beach ball bounces and drags my friend,
He yells, "I swear, this isn't my end!"

I spot a crab that scuttles away,
It dances like it's in a cabaret.
We clapped and cheered for its grand ballet,
Who knew crustaceans could have such sway?

Sunshine winks, amidst giggles and snacks,
Bikini blunders and sandy backs.
We laugh till we cry, with smiles so bright,
Our day's an adventure, a pure delight.

As waves wrap gently around our feet,
We promise next time, we'll bring more treats.
Sunlit dreams we'll savor forevermore,
In memories we crash on laughter's shore.

Kaleidoscope of the Coastal Breeze

The sun was shining, oh so bright,
As seagulls danced in playful flight.
A coconut dropped with a thud,
Turns out it's not a beachside bud!

Laughter rolled across the sand,
While crabs waltzed, holding hands.
A beach ball hit a sunbather's snack,
Now there's a sandwich under attack!

The sunscreen bottle made a run,
As kids chased after it for fun.
But slippery hands and squeals of glee,
Created chaos by the sea!

With flip-flops flinging left and right,
We laughed until the fading light.
In the breeze, we found our groove,
A coastal carnival that made us move!

Shadows Weaving Through Dreams

In the afternoon, the sun would play,
Casting shadows in a quirky display.
A lizard skittered, took a dive,
Just trying hard to feel alive!

A picnic spread, oh what a feast,
Till ants arrived, the unexpected beast.
They marched in line, an army bold,
Taking our snacks was their goal untold!

A towel flew high, a gust did blow,
Landing on a stranger, oh what a show!
With laughter echoing through the breeze,
We giggled harder, as we aimed to please.

The sunset glowed, we danced around,
With laughter and joy, our hearts were found.
This day of pranks, we can't forget,
In shadows woven, we still laugh yet!

Beneath Whispering Fronds

Underneath the leafy green,
A squirrel darted, quick and keen.
He snatched a chip, how very bold,
With a cheeky grin, his tale was told!

Beneath the fronds, we built a fort,
Our giggles echoed, a wild sport.
But the wind came through with a sudden whoosh,
Making our fort a big ol' swoosh!

As drinks spilled out with fizzling cheer,
A raccoon visited, seeking beer.
We laughed and shared the day's delight,
While wild tales took off into the night!

With sandy toes and salty waves,
Our mischief bloomed, our spirit saves.
In the shade, our hearts stayed free,
Underneath the fronds, just you and me!

Dappled Dreams at Dusk

As twilight came, the sky turned pink,
We gathered shells, and then we stank!
With tide pools full of octopus hand,
We found the weirdest in the sand!

A starfish winked with a silly grin,
We pondered if it could swim or spin.
With laughter bubbling, waves came right,
So much fun, it felt so light!

The beach ball bounced with goofy flair,
Soon tangled up in a beachgoer's hair.
We roared with laughter, the scene was grand,
Who knew the evening would be so planned?

As dusk descended, we danced like fools,
With twinkling stars, our heartfelt jewels.
In dappled dreams, carefree we thrived,
A joyful night where fun arrived!

www.ingramcontent.com/pod-product-compliance
Lightning Source LLC
Chambersburg PA
CBHW050317100526
44585CB00016BA/1559